DINOSAURS: FACT AND FABLE

TRUTHS, MYTHS, AND NEW DISCOVERIES!

SEYMOUR SIMON

HARPER

An Imprint of HarperCollinsPublishers

For kids who love dinosaurs so much they know how to spell (and pronounce) Compsognathus . . . and many other dinosaurs. I did too.

Special thanks to Dr. Stephen Brusatte.

Dinosaurs: Fact and Fable
Copyright © 2020 by Seymour Simon
All rights reserved. Manufactured in Italy.
No part of this book may be used or reproduced in any manner whatsoever without written permission
except in the case of brief quotations embodied in critical articles and reviews. For information address
HarperCollins Children's Books, a division of HarperCollins Publishers, 195 Broadway, New York, NY 10007.
www.harpercollinschildrens.com

Library of Congress Control Number: 2019953362
ISBN 978-0-06-247064-5 (trade bdg.) — ISBN 978-0-06-247063-8 (pbk.)

Typography by Brenda E. Angelilli
Photo Research by Liz Nealon
20 21 22 23 24 RTLO 10 9 8 7 6 5 4 3 2 1
❖
First Edition

AUTHOR'S NOTE

When I was younger, I learned many incorrect things about dinosaurs. I read that most dinosaurs were giant armored reptiles that moved sluggishly through an ancient jungle world or were feeble-minded beasts just waiting around to become extinct. The dinosaurs I saw were enormous fossil skeletons at museums like the American Museum of Natural History or pictured in monster movies such as *One Million B.C.,* in which early humans battled dinosaurs with spears and arrows.

Thankfully, in the years that followed, many new discoveries were made! We found out that dinosaurs were not all giant-sized: Some were quite small—about the size of a cat or a dog. They were not all slow-moving: Some could move very quickly, like a lion charging or a wolf hunting. A whole group of dinosaurs even developed feathers and wings.

As much as we've learned over the years, we are still making discoveries with many remaining questions about dinosaurs. My hope is that this book teaches you some new dinosaur facts, fables, and findings. Welcome to the wonderful world of dinosaurs!

Seymour Simon at the American Museum of Natural History doing research for this book.

DIGGING DEEP FOR DINOSAURS

Finding out about dinosaurs for a scientist is like solving a mystery for a detective. In both cases, they look for clues. Detectives study clues such as fingerprints, DNA, or any evidence that'll help them crack the case. For **paleontologists**, scientists who study dinosaurs and other ancient creatures, the evidence they search for are fossils, and their goal is to investigate dinosaurs.

Paleontologists have learned many fascinating things both from fossils that were discovered over 100 years ago and ones that were discovered during your lifetime. From the deserts of the southwest United States and Argentina to ice fields in Alaska and vast areas in China, nowadays a new species of dinosaur is being discovered almost every week. That's about 50 new species of dinosaurs being discovered every year.

Before, scientists used tools such as chisels and brushes to examine fossils. But now they have new ways of studying the fossils: using electronic scanners, high-powered microscopes, and computer programs. In this book, we'll explore some clues in the mystery of the dinosaurs by looking back at some of the older findings as well as introducing newer ones.

After reading this book, perhaps one of you will go on to become a science detective and help solve the many mysteries of the dinosaurs.

WHAT ARE DINOSAURS?

Dinosaurs are a group of prehistoric reptiles that lived on Earth beginning about 231 million years ago. The common dinosaurs we know became extinct about 66 million years ago, although paleontologists discovered that birds living today evolved from and are dinosaurs.

There was a lot of diversity among dinosaurs. Some dinosaurs were huge, weighing up to 80 tons, about as much as four fully loaded school buses. Others were the size of a chicken and weighed only a few pounds.

Dinosaurs were different from all other reptiles because of the positioning of their legs. Lizards, alligators, and other modern-day reptiles have legs that sprawl out to their sides. Dinosaurs' legs extended straight out below their bodies, allowing them to stand, walk, or run upright.

Fan-fingered gecko, a modern-day reptile

CARNOTAURUS

AUCASAURUS

COELOPHYSIS

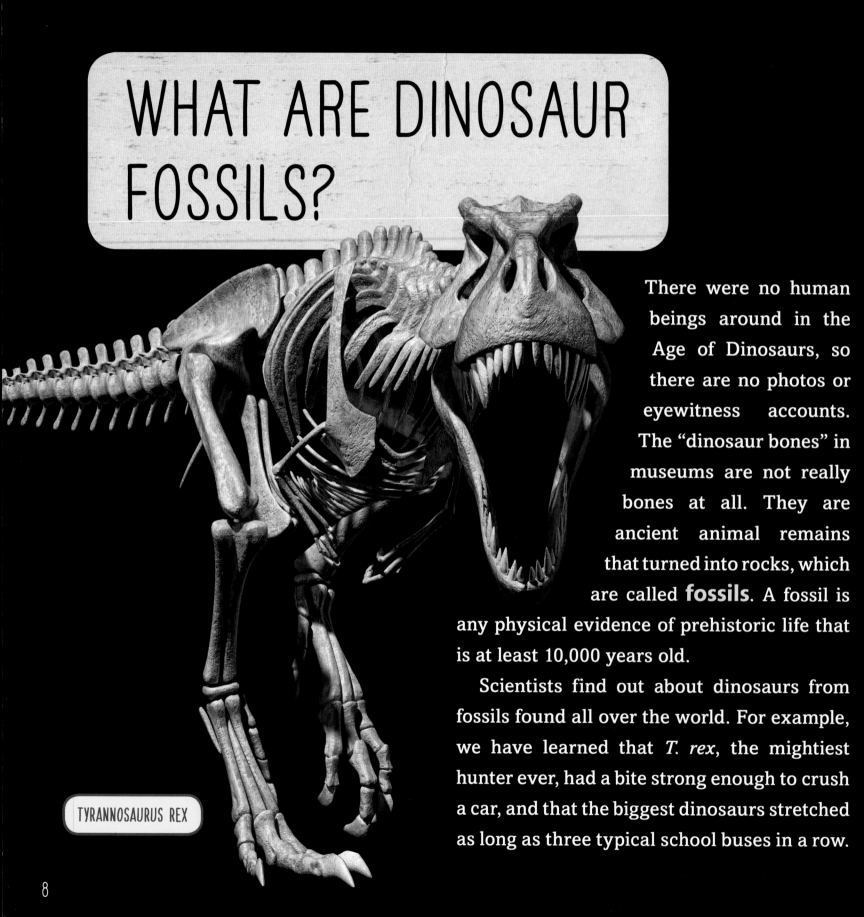

WHAT ARE DINOSAUR FOSSILS?

There were no human beings around in the Age of Dinosaurs, so there are no photos or eyewitness accounts. The "dinosaur bones" in museums are not really bones at all. They are ancient animal remains that turned into rocks, which are called **fossils**. A fossil is any physical evidence of prehistoric life that is at least 10,000 years old.

Scientists find out about dinosaurs from fossils found all over the world. For example, we have learned that *T. rex*, the mightiest hunter ever, had a bite strong enough to crush a car, and that the biggest dinosaurs stretched as long as three typical school buses in a row.

TYRANNOSAURUS REX

Trace fossil of the footprint of an *Iguanodontid* dinosaur, a herbivore that lived during the Cretaceous period.

Note: The dino-print is many times larger than the human foot next to it.

DIGGING DEEPER

Because they are science detectives looking at 100-million-year-old clues, sometimes paleontologists have to go beyond fossils to figure out how dinosaurs lived. Many also look at dinosaurs' closest living relatives, such as crocodiles and birds. For example, they measured the biting force of a crocodile's jaws at about 3,700 pounds, the strongest bite on record for a living animal. Because a *T. rex*'s jaws were more than twice as big as a crocodile's, paleontologists can estimate that the bite of a *T. rex* is nearly twice as strong as a crocodile's.

TYPES OF FOSSILS

The most commonly discovered fossils are rocks that form over time from the preserved bones and teeth of dinosaurs. These are called **body fossils**. Fossils of footprints, skin impressions, and eggs have been discovered as well. These are called **trace fossils**. Fossils are sometimes found on the ground in places where no one has looked before, but most fossils are normally dug up from underground caves, ashfall from volcanoes, ancient oceans, riverbeds, and tar pits.

THE EARLIEST DINOSAUR DISCOVERIES

Richard Owen standing next to a reconstructed skeleton of the *Dinornis maximus*, the largest of the extinct, wingless birds that lived in what is now New Zealand.

In 1841, nearly 200 years ago, the British biologist, anatomist, and paleontologist Richard Owen was the first person to use the term "dinosaurs." Owen's research focused on the fossilized remains of three giant reptiles, the hunter *Megalosaurus*, a plant-eater named *Iguanodon*, and a heavily armored reptile named *Hylaeosaurus*.

Owen noticed that the three giant reptiles shared a few features with one another but not with any other animals. He noted that unlike the common lizard, the creatures' giant legs were upright and extended straight to the ground beneath their bodies. He also saw that each of the animals had five vertebrae (small bones forming the backbone) fused together and attached to the pelvis (the base of the spine). He classified them as a new group of animals, which he named Dinosauria, derived from ancient Greek words meaning "terrible lizard (or reptile)."

A FIRST FIND

One of the first dinosaurs found was the *Eoraptor* (meaning "dawn stealer"), so named because scientists believed it lived at the dawn of the Age of Dinosaurs. It was about the size of a large dog and was an omnivore, which means it ate meat and plants.

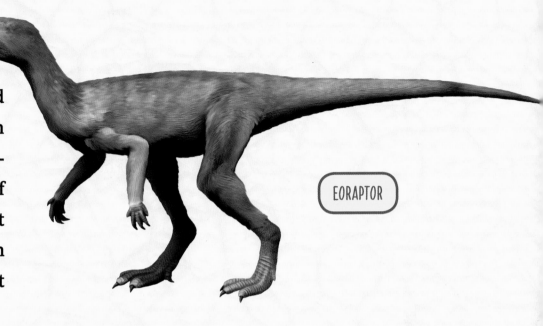

EORAPTOR

MARY ANNING, FOSSIL HUNTER

Mary Anning (1799–1847) was one of the first fossil hunters. She made animal fossil discoveries at the same time as Owen. However, she often did not receive credit for her work because she was poor and a woman. Most scientists at that time were men from wealthy families.

A NEW DEFINITION OF DINOSAURS

STYGIMOLOCH

Dinosauria is too general to describe the diversity of this prehistoric group of reptiles. With each new fossil discovery, we get a different criterion for which features make up a dinosaur, so the definition of "dinosaur" is not so clear-cut. Dinosaurs had body differences that set them apart from other reptiles. We simply don't know what all those features were.

Yet there are some basic rules that paleontologists agree can help us decide which ancient animals were dinosaurs:

- *Dinosaurs lived mostly on land between 231 and 66 million years ago.*
- *They had legs that stretched straight down from their bodies.*
- *They were reptiles.*

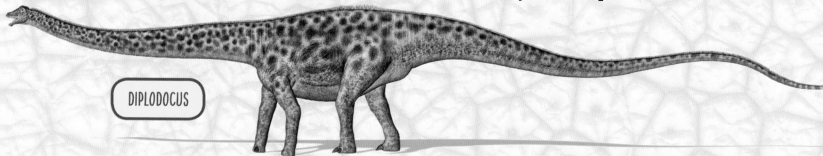

DIPLODOCUS

An accurate and up-to-date definition of a dinosaur is very general. Here it is:

A FOSSILIZED REPTILE OF THE MESOZOIC ERA, OFTEN VERY LARGE AND MOSTLY LAND DWELLING, THAT EATS PLANTS OR ANIMALS.

WHEN DINOSAURS ROAMED THE EARTH

(A TIMELINE)

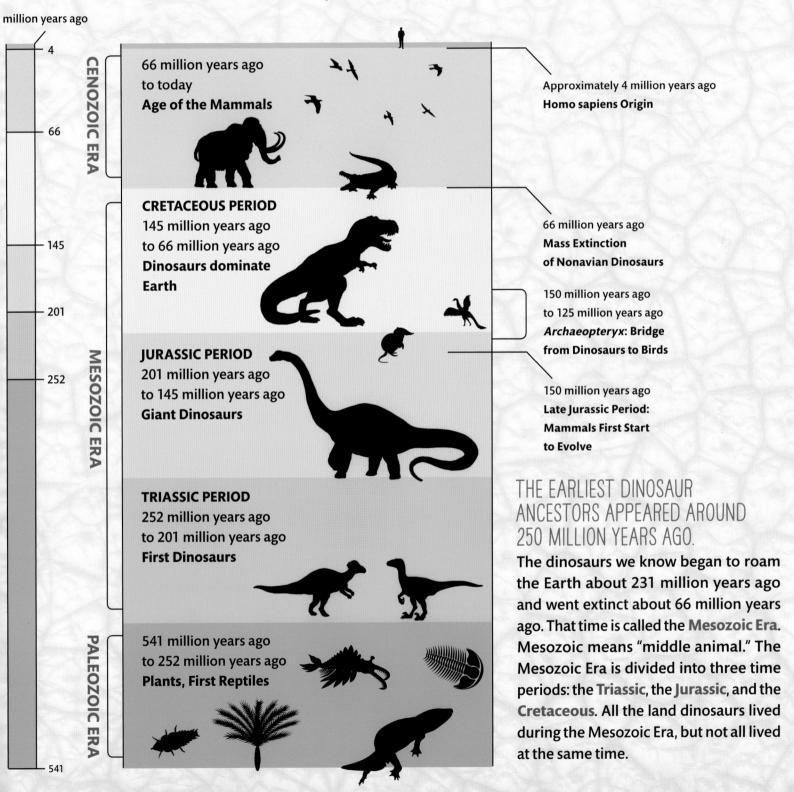

million years ago

4

66

145

201

252

541

CENOZOIC ERA

MESOZOIC ERA

PALEOZOIC ERA

66 million years ago
to today
Age of the Mammals

CRETACEOUS PERIOD
145 million years ago
to 66 million years ago
**Dinosaurs dominate
Earth**

JURASSIC PERIOD
201 million years ago
to 145 million years ago
Giant Dinosaurs

TRIASSIC PERIOD
252 million years ago
to 201 million years ago
First Dinosaurs

541 million years ago
to 252 million years ago
Plants, First Reptiles

Approximately 4 million years ago
Homo sapiens Origin

66 million years ago
**Mass Extinction
of Nonavian Dinosaurs**

150 million years ago
to 125 million years ago
Archaeopteryx: **Bridge
from Dinosaurs to Birds**

150 million years ago
**Late Jurassic Period:
Mammals First Start
to Evolve**

THE EARLIEST DINOSAUR
ANCESTORS APPEARED AROUND
250 MILLION YEARS AGO.

The dinosaurs we know began to roam
the Earth about 231 million years ago
and went extinct about 66 million years
ago. That time is called the **Mesozoic Era**.
Mesozoic means "middle animal." The
Mesozoic Era is divided into three time
periods: the **Triassic**, the **Jurassic**, and the
Cretaceous. All the land dinosaurs lived
during the Mesozoic Era, but not all lived
at the same time.

13

We don't know for sure what *Velociraptors* ate, but, as shown in this artwork, it is likely that this turkey-sized dinosaur would have eaten rodent-sized mammals.

EARLY MAMMALS

The first **mammals**, warm-blooded animals that care for their young, appeared at the end of the Triassic Period and existed with the dinosaurs throughout the Mesozoic Era. Early mammals, such as the shrewlike *Morganucodon*, were mostly small animals, often only a few inches long and a few ounces in weight, about the size of a mouse. *Morganucodon* fed on insects and plants and could escape either up trees or down into burrows when bigger meat-eating dinosaurs stomped nearby.

HOT-BLOODED, COLD-BLOODED, AND IN BETWEEN

Mammals are **hot-blooded**. The terms "hot-blooded" or "warm-blooded" are determined by an animal's ability to keep a constant body temperature despite variations in the temperature of its surroundings. Mammals' internal warmth, furry or hairy bodies, and tiny sizes helped them to survive when Earth's temperatures plummeted and plant food became scarce.

Unlike modern-day reptiles, large dinosaurs were probably **heterotherms**, meaning animals whose body temperatures change depending on their activities. Scientists are still not certain of this, but they know that dinosaurs definitely grew faster and were more active than today's cold-blooded amphibians and reptiles.

WHAT WOULD A SCIENTIST SAY?

Scientists use more technical terms for hot- and cold-blooded:

ECTOTHERMS
(cold-blooded):
Animals that depend upon their surroundings and behavior to regulate body temperature, such as reptiles and fish. The body temperatures of fish are usually very close to the water they live in.

ENDOTHERMS
(hot-blooded):
Animals that generate internal heat to keep their body temperature constant, such as birds and mammals.

HETEROTHERMS
(other-temperatured):
Some animals, such as bumblebees, certain bats and squirrels, and a few fish species, show properties of both groups.

WHERE DID DINOSAURS LIVE?

At the beginning of the Age of Dinosaurs, all the continents were linked together in a single landmass called **Pangaea**. During the millions of years that dinosaurs existed, Pangaea slowly broke apart and its pieces spread around the world into the modern arrangement of continents by a process called **plate tectonics**. Dinosaurs lived on all the continents.

Many dinosaur fossils and the greatest number of dinosaur species have been found in the high deserts and badlands of North America, China, and Argentina. Deserts have few plants, and that prevented fossils from being covered by decaying plants over centuries of time, making them easier to find.

A WARM ANTARCTICA?

Dinosaur fossils have been found on all the modern continents, including Antarctica. During the Early Jurassic Period, Antarctica was 600 miles closer to the equator and it had temperate forests teeming with small mammals, winged reptiles, and both plant-eating and meat-eating dinosaurs.

Illustration of a pair of sparring *Cryolophosaurus* under the lights of the aurora australis, the southern equivalent of the aurora borealis (northern lights).

Earth, 250 million years ago: All land was part of a supercontinent called Pangaea.

Triassic Period, 200 million years ago: Pangaea broke into two parts, Laurasia (north) and Gondwanaland (south).

Jurassic Period, 145 million years ago: What would become South America and Africa are still close together; other continents are drifting apart.

Cretaceous Period, 66 million years ago: South America and Africa have separated.

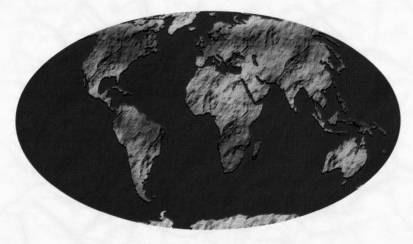

Earth today.

HOW DO DINOSAURS GET THEIR NAMES?

All animals and plants, whether living or extinct, are given a scientific name. Their discoverers are scientists who name them by following a set of rules called the International Code of Zoological Nomenclature. The scientific name of a certain dinosaur ensures that all paleontologists are talking about the same animal.

The code says that a scientific designation is composed of two names. The first name, called the genus, always starts with a capital letter. The second name, called the species, is never capitalized. Thus, we have names for dinosaurs such as *Tyrannosaurus rex*, *Brontosaurus excelsus*, and *Triceratops horridus*. Sometimes the genus name is abbreviated, such as in *T. rex* for *Tyrannosaurus rex*. Other times the genus name alone may be used to refer to all the species in a genus, such as *Brontosaurus* or *Triceratops*.

A paleontologist who discovers a new dinosaur often uses names that come from Greek or Latin words. Some names tell us where the fossil was collected or who collected it or highlight the dinosaur's unusual features. Thus, the name *Triceratops* comes from Greek words meaning "three-horned face." *Utahraptor* and *Denversaurus* were named after the state of Utah and the city of Denver, respectively.

Illustration of a *Tyrannosaurus rex* and a *Triceratops* in a classic face-off.

DINO-MITE DISCOVERIES

A baby *Udanoceratops* hatching from an egg.

After nearly 200 years of discoveries, we know more about dinosaurs than ever before. Yet we are still refining our ideas about how they looked, behaved, and lived.

BABY DINOSAURS

All dinosaurs hatched from fertilized eggs laid by female dinosaurs. Dinosaur mothers laid clutches of anywhere from ten eggs to dozens at a time in nests. The eggs had hard, brittle shells like those of modern-day birds. Dinosaur eggs were round or oval and ranged from golf-ball-sized to about two feet long.

Even the biggest dinosaurs, such as *T. rex*, probably started off as relatively small eggs, not much bigger than a grapefruit. By examining the growth patterns in cross-sections of their body fossils, scientists think that a baby *T. rex* gained about 4.5 pounds a day and over 1,600 pounds a year until its teenage years. An adult *T. rex* weighed over 15,000 pounds, about as much as five compact cars. Compare that growth rate to a modern crocodile, which grows very slowly and to a much smaller adult size and weight, about 15 to 20 feet long and 2,500 pounds.

A baby *Tyrannosaurus rex* roars. It is easy to act tough when you are standing safely between your eight-ton mother's legs.

HOW LONG DID DINOSAURS LIVE?

In the early days of paleontology, most scientists thought that dinosaurs grew slowly and didn't become adults for decades. But scientific research nowadays proves otherwise. Using advanced electron microscopes to look at the cell structure of dinosaur bones has resulted in more precise answers to this question. Paleontologists measure slices of fossils to determine the speed of growth of the animal's bones.

Like cross-sections of tree trunks, where the spaces between the growth rings show how quickly or slowly the tree was growing, the large white spaces in this cross-sectional slice of a dinosaur bone (above) show that it was a fast-growing bone. This suggests that dinosaurs did not live very long (perhaps only 30 years), compared to today's reptiles, which can live as long as a century.

BRACHIOSAURUS

HOW FAST COULD A DINOSAUR RUN?

We know that dinosaurs moved; all animals do. But did they move slowly like turtles or run fast like cheetahs? A dinosaur's size, shape, and structure can give us clues as to how fast it may have moved.

The trails of footprints, or **dinosaur tracks**, can also give scientists a rough guess of how fast a dinosaur was moving at a particular moment. The tracking method involves measuring the size of each footprint and the distance between each print. The fastest speeds we have found measuring a trackway of dinosaur footprints is about 20 miles per hour, which is faster than most humans can run.

A running pack of carnivorous *Compsognathus* dinosaurs.

An *Anchiornis huxleyi* fossil with its feather imprints clearly visible. As shown in the illustration, the *Anchiornis* was a small and feathered dinosaur that weighed only about a quarter of a pound.

WHAT COLORS WERE DINOSAURS?

In the past, most dinosaurs were colored gray or green in paintings and in books, but recently dinosaurs have been pictured differently—with a variety of bright colors and patterns. So, what color *were* they? We might have a clue.

Fossils of small, feathered dinosaurs have been found in Early Cretaceous Period rock in China. Just a few years ago, scientists discovered tiny structures called **melanosomes** within the fossilized feathers of dinosaurs closely related to

birds. Today, scientists know that different kinds of melanosomes produced specific colors in a dinosaur's appearance.

Melanosomes were also found in other small dinosaur fossils. The fossil of a chicken-sized dinosaur named *Anchiornis* not only showed clear imprints of feathers, it also had traces of melanosomes that led scientists to conclude that it was clearly multicolored and probably had black-and-white-striped wings and a brown crest of feathers.

BETTER TO EAT WITH!

The earliest finds of dinosaur fossils were dinosaur teeth. At that time, some people thought they were dragon teeth. Since then, paleontologists have studied the size and shape of these fossils to learn how and what dinosaurs ate.

Some dinosaurs were **meat-eaters** and had sharp ripping teeth to help them cut into their prey. Other kinds of dinosaurs (commonly known as **plant-eaters**) had grinding teeth for eating plants.

Some dinosaurs did not have any teeth at all. Avian (birdlike) dinosaurs had beaks and ate small insects and plant parts. Paleontologists believe that, like birds today, these dinosaurs ground up what they ate with their hard beaks or just digested them in their stomachs.

CAN YOU FIND A DINOSAUR FOSSIL?

While it's possible for anyone to find a dinosaur fossil in some untouched, little-explored spot where few people live, most dinosaur fossils are found by paleontologists digging into layers of **sedimentary rocks**. Sedimentary rocks form over many centuries when sand, mud, and dead organisms settle onto the muddy bottoms of oceans, lakes, rivers, beaches, and other bodies of water. Over time, they are squeezed together by their weight to form layers of sedimentary bedrock.

Rock hammers, chisels, and other tools are used to remove layers of rock until a fossil is found. As a broken fossil bone or skeleton is found, layers of special glue are used to hold the fossils together. Next a trench is dug around the fossil so that it sits surrounded by rock. Then the entire fossil and rock surrounding are shipped back to a

museum, where workers carefully remove the fossil from the surrounding rock. Finally the workers use glues and fillers to keep the fossil together.

So can you or anyone else find a dinosaur fossil? Yes! After all, the youngest person to find a new dinosaur species was only seven years old at the time. With your family or friends, you can possibly find one in likely places, such as spots where other dinosaur fossils have been found nearby, in a layer of sedimentary rock.

SAFETY FIRST:
Wear protective goggles and clothing and have an adult with you who knows how and what to do.

MYSTERIES DECODED

There are still many things we don't know about dinosaurs, but we find more answers to our questions every day. Here are some of the answers that paleontologists have proposed to crack some dinosaur cases.

HOW ARE DINOSAURS LIKE BIRDS?

Most dinosaurs looked and behaved more like birds than lizards. Many dinosaurs had feathers and laid eggs, and their body parts (brain, heart, and skeleton) were quite similar to those of birds. Today's birds aren't distant relatives of dinosaurs; they are dinosaurs in the same way bats are mammals.

OSTRICH

WERE SAUROPODS THE BIGGEST LAND ANIMAL THAT EVER LIVED?

Probably, say most scientists. Sauropods were giant dinosaurs with very long necks, long tails, small heads, and four thick, treelike feet. So far there have not been any larger land animal fossils found.

PTERODACTYL

HOW MANY KINDS OF DINOSAURS WERE THERE?

The dinosaur family is usually divided into two main groups: Saurischian (lizard-hipped) dinosaurs (such as predators *T. rex* and sauropods such as *Brontosaurus*) and Ornithischian (bird-hipped) dinosaurs (such as *Stegosaurus*).

WERE ALL GIANT ANIMALS DINOSAURS?

During the Age of Dinosaurs, some of the larger animals were not dinosaurs at all. *Pterodactyls* were sizable flying lizards that lived during the Age of Dinosaurs, but they were not dinosaurs. Plesiosaurs were large ocean reptiles that lived in the Age of Dinosaurs, but likewise they were not part of the dinosaur family.

DINO-STARS

There are many kinds of dinosaurs—some more popular than others. Here are some of the most well-known and well-liked dinosaurs. Everyone probably has a favorite dinosaur. What's yours?

TYRANNOSAURUS REX

Tyrannosaurus rex (Greek words for "tyrant lizard" and the Latin word for "king") is the largest meat-eating dinosaur that ever lived. *T. rex* lived in the forested lands of western North America during the Late Cretaceous Period, about 66 million years ago. Fossils of *T. rex* show that it was about 40 feet long and 15 to 20 feet tall, and it weighed up to seven tons. It had strong hind feet and a long, powerful tail that helped it run at about 10 to 20 miles an hour.

That means that there was a chance a *T. rex* could catch a human being in an imaginary race. It was certainly fast enough to catch and eat other dinosaurs, such as *Triceratops*. When it caught its prey, *T. rex* used large, sawlike teeth to pierce and rip through flesh. From roots to tips, its teeth were about a foot long. It had two-fingered front forelimbs that might have helped seize a prey animal, but they were probably too short to reach its mouth. Paleontologists know that *T. rex* crushed through bones as it ate; broken-bone fossils of its prey have been found in its fossilized remains.

31

TRICERATOPS

Like *T. rex*, *Triceratops* (Greek words for "three-horned face") lived in the Late Cretaceous Period. *Triceratops* is easily recognized because of its large size, three horns, and the frill around its head. A fully grown adult was about 30 feet long and weighed around ten tons, as much as two heavy dump trucks. Its skull was huge, measuring over seven feet long. *Triceratops* ate plants and had between 400 and 800 teeth. Its horns were probably used to defend against attacks by *T. rex* and as display structures to attract mates.

Triceratops is so popular that it's the state dinosaur of Wyoming. This dinosaur also appears in the

VELOCIRAPTOR

This small dinosaur was about six feet long and 1.6 feet in height at the hip, and it weighed about 30 to 35 pounds. *Velociraptor* (Greek words meaning "speedy thief") lived in the Late Cretaceous Period, about 75 million years ago. The first known fossil of its kind was found in the Gobi Desert of China and Mongolia in 1922.

It was fast, able to run up to 40 miles per hour in short bursts, and it had a sharp, sickle-shaped claw on each foot. The claws were probably used for grabbing its prey and to help climb trees. *Velociraptor* didn't fly, but it probably had feathers covering its legs and body.

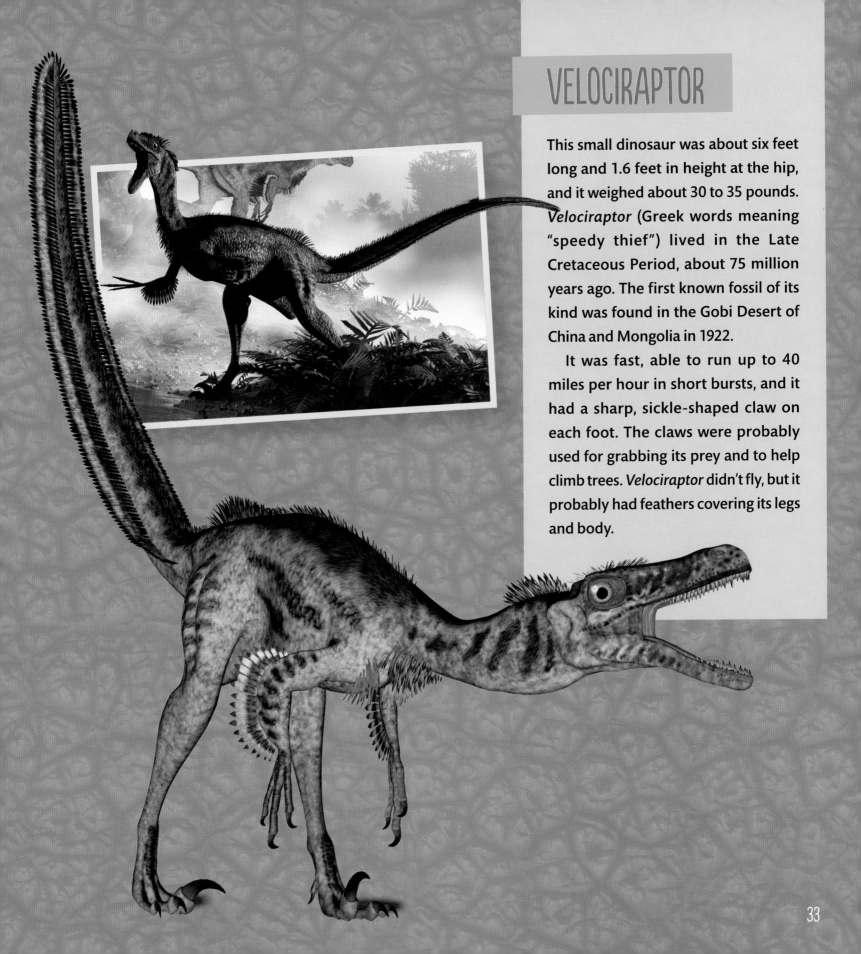

BRONTOSAURUS

Although well known by many people, *Brontosaurus* (Greek words meaning "thunder lizard") has long been thought to have been misnamed. Since 1903, scientists thought the *Brontosaurus* fossils were in fact the same as another dinosaur group called *Apatosaurus*. But a long and detailed study of 81 different sets of fossils, which was published in 2015, found that the original *Apatosaurus* and *Brontosaurus* fossils are different enough to be in separate groups after all. So the *Brontosaurus* is back!

Both species were members of a family of dinosaurs called sauropods that walked on four legs and had long necks and long tails, small heads with blunt teeth, and a small brain. They had huge guts, which were needed because they ate large amounts of plants.

The largest species of *Brontosaurus*, *B. excelsus*, was about 15 feet high at its hips, had a length of about 70 feet, and weighed about 30,000 pounds.

STEGOSAURUS

Stegosaurus comes from Greek words meaning "roofed lizard." That's because the *Stegosaurus* had armored plates along its back that overlapped like the shingles on a roof. *Stegosaurus* had one of the smallest dinosaur brains, only the size of two walnuts—tiny for a dinosaur that was 30 feet long and weighed over four tons. It lived about 155 million years ago, during the Late Jurassic Period. A slow-moving, plant-eating dinosaur, *Stegosaurus* had a rounded back and a double row of spikes on its tail.

Colorado's nickname is the "Stegosaurus State" because the first *Stegosaurus* fossil was found there. Along with *T. rex*, *Stegosaurus* was one of the dinosaurs that inspired the fictional dinosaur Godzilla, who was the ferocious star of movies, TV shows, comics, and video games.

THE BIGGEST DINOSAUR

The largest dinosaur ever found so far is a plant-eater named *Patagotitan mayorum*. The first part of its name refers to the Patagonian region of Argentina, where the fossils were found. The second half of the name honors the Mayo family, who owned the land where the dinosaur was discovered.

Patagotitan lived about 100 million years ago, during the Cretaceous Period. It is the largest member in a family of giant dinosaurs called titanosaurs. One of its fossilized thigh bones was eight feet from end to end and it weighed anywhere from 120,000 to 160,000 pounds—about the weight of a dozen or more African bush elephants.

These giant dinosaurs had tails over 40 feet long. The long tails worked like a bike stand to keep the long-necked dinosaurs in balance. A 122-foot-long model of *P. mayorum* went on display at the American Museum of Natural History in New York City in January 2016.

human height

THE NOT-SO-BIGGEST DINOSAURS

Not all dinosaurs were very, very big. Some were medium-sized, and others small. One of the smallest sets of dinosaur fossils ever found was *Compsognathus*. Its name means "fancy-jawed." It lived during the Late Jurassic Period, about 150 million years ago, in what is now Europe.

Compsognathus was about the size of a chicken, and it was like a bird in some other ways as well. Its body was covered with feathers. It had a short neck, strong hind legs, and very small arms. It was a swift runner on its hind legs and hunted small animals for food.

More recently, an even smaller, related dinosaur was discovered in China. The dinosaur was named *Sinosauropteryx*. It weighed a bit less than its cousin *Compsognathus* and was also covered in feathers. One fossil also showed the remains of a lizard and some small mammals in its stomach. Another fossil contained several chicken-sized eggs, which scientists think were the dinosaur's own, unlaid eggs.

SINOSAUROPTERYX

NEW DINOSAUR DISCOVERIES

We're living in the golden age of dinosaur discoveries. Illinois-born Stephen Brusatte, a professor at the University of Edinburgh in Scotland, has named more than a dozen new dinosaur species. Brusatte believes that new technologies such as electron microscopes and **CT scans** are changing the way paleontologists study fossils.

In recent years, huge numbers of fossils have been unearthed in China. A rock formation north of Beijing is a hot spot of recent finds, containing Early Cretaceous Period fossils, including detailed remains of feathered dinosaurs like *Sinosauropteryx*. These findings have made scientists more closely examine the relationship between dinosaurs and birds.

Western North America is another one of the best places to find new dinosaur fossils. A sedimentary rock layer called the Morrison Formation in the western United States from Montana to New Mexico is where many fossils, including early digs of *Stegosaurus* and *Apatosaurus*, were found. Dinosaur National Monument (a US national park), located on the border of Utah and Colorado, remains a great place to look for dinosaur fossils. Others are found from the southwest United States all the way north through Canada. Scientists are still finding complete fossilized skeletons of dinosaurs in digs from Texas to Montana. Over 50 different kinds of dinosaurs have been discovered in Canada's Dinosaur Provincial Park in Alberta.

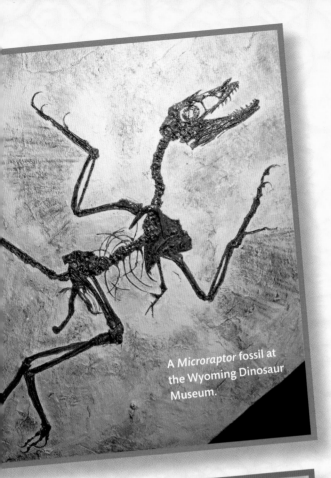

A *Microraptor* fossil at the Wyoming Dinosaur Museum.

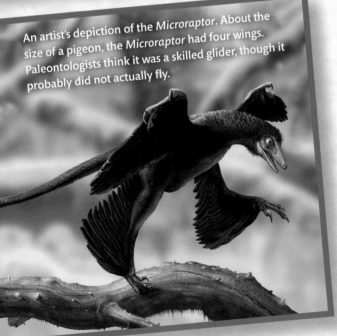

An artist's depiction of the *Microraptor*. About the size of a pigeon, the *Microraptor* had four wings. Paleontologists think it was a skilled glider, though it probably did not actually fly.

JINGMAI O'CONNOR

Jingmai O'Connor, an American paleontologist who lives and works in China, is a worldwide expert in feathered dinosaurs. Along with her colleague Xing Xu, she analyzed the remains of a *Microraptor* and found the bones of a small bird in its gut, concluding that the dinosaurs ate birds.

LITTLE PEOPLE, BIG FINDS

The youngest person ever to find a new dinosaur species was seven-year-old Diego Suárez. In 2004, he was playing in the forests of Aysén, Chile, when he found the fossil of a new dinosaur (pictured above). His parents were geologists and they realized he had found something important. The species was later named *Chilesaurus diegosuarezi* in honor of his discovery.

WHAT HAPPENED TO THE DINOSAURS?

For more than 160 million years, dinosaurs roamed planet Earth. Then, 66 million years ago, every nonbird dinosaur, small and large, plant-eater and meat-eater, died out. Many other animals disappeared about the same time, including pterosaurs (flying reptiles) and plesiosaurs (giant swimming reptiles). Other animal families as well as plankton (the bottom of the ocean food chain) and plants of all kinds were hard hit.

However, other animals living during the Age of Dinosaurs survived, including crocodiles, turtles, cockroaches, and some mammals and birds. Why did so many species become extinct yet others survived to modern times? That's a mystery that has puzzled scientists since dinosaurs were first discovered.

Scientists know that there was a global climate change 66 million years ago, and the climate shifted from warm to cool. They have also found a thin dark line, called the **K-T boundary**, that formed at the same time in layers of sedimentary rocks around the world. The climate change and the K-T boundary line must have something to do with why the dinosaurs died. But what happened exactly? And how did it bring an end to the Age of Dinosaurs?

TWO EXTINCTION THEORIES

Today two main theories, or hypotheses, exist in paleontology about what caused the end of the Age of Dinosaurs, otherwise known as the **mass extinction** event of the species. One is called the **asteroid explanation**. The other is called the **volcano explanation**. Paleontologists have already discredited many other ideas, such as that dinosaurs were too stupid to survive, or that they devoured their own eggs and young and ate themselves into extinction. The two current main theories share certain clues:

1. There was global climate change. The causes and how fast the climate changed are the main differences between the two theories.

2. Many species other than the dinosaurs became extinct.

3. There is a thin layer of the rare metal **iridium**, the fallout from the asteroid, near the K-T boundary.

THE ASTEROID THEORY

The asteroid theory was first proposed in 1980 by Walter and Luis Alvarez. Walter was a professor of Earth and Planetary Science at the University of California, Berkeley. Luis, Walter's father, was a Nobel Prize–winning physicist. Their original theory stated that a large asteroid or other space object crashed into Earth, throwing up a huge cloud of dust that caused a change in climate and the extinction of dinosaurs.

Eleven years after the Alvarezes proposed their theory, an approximate 100-mile crater was found at Chicxulub on the Yucatán Peninsula of Mexico. It fit their predictions exactly. Shocked quartz rocks and glassy spheres (both formed by a huge asteroid impact) as well as a soot layer (evidence of countless forest fires) were found at the K-T boundary in many places. The asteroid theory says that all these changes are the result of a large space object's impact with planet Earth.

Scientists have discovered new evidence that the impact of the asteroid was as powerful as ten billion World War II–era atomic bombs. The asteroid crash may have caused 75% of life over the entire world to become extinct. The crash may have triggered wildfires over 900 miles away, as well as causing a tremendous, destructive tsunami.

THE VOLCANO THEORY

Some scientists agree that the asteroid crash happened but believe the extinction of the dinosaurs was of an earthly nature and more gradual. Evidence shows that in the five million years leading up to the K-T extinction, Earth saw a huge burst of volcanic eruptions. The eruptions gave off enormous amounts of choking, sunlight-blocking volcanic ash, having a disastrous effect all over the world. Over time, the repeated volcanic eruptions released large amounts of dust, sulfur, and carbon dioxide in addition to the ash. The theory claims the eruptions acidified Earth's oceans and caused climate change over millions of years, weakening the dinosaurs to the point that they died when an asteroid crashed into the Yucatán.

WHICH DO SCIENTISTS BELIEVE?

The exact cause of the mass extinction of the dinosaurs remains a mystery. So far neither theory fully explains what killed the dinosaurs. Neither theory really explains why certain animals died while others survived. It's also not certain from the fossil record whether there was a sudden catastrophe or a gradual decline in an animal species.

The same evidence is used by both sides to prove a different point. In the end, one theory does not prove the other wrong. Some scientists believe perhaps both events happened and collectively contributed to the end of the dinosaurs.

ARE PRESENT-DAY BIRDS *REALLY* DINOSAURS?

Strange as it may sound, paleontologists agree that birds are avian dinosaurs and part of the **theropod** family. Theropods are a kind of dinosaur with hollow bones and three-toed feet.

Of course, modern-day birds are quite different from the dinosaurs that lived millions of years ago. Over centuries, the environment changes, and birds, like all other forms of life, change too. Present-day birds have changed so that they look, act, and function very differently than dinosaurs. Still, think about it:

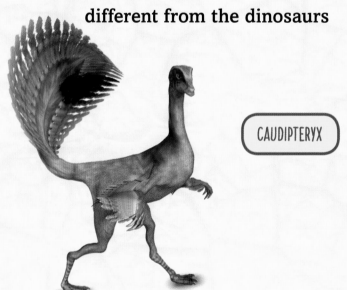

CAUDIPTERYX

WHEN YOU SEE AN EAGLE OR A HAWK DIVE DOWN OUT OF THE SKY TO SNATCH A FISH FROM A LAKE, OR A CHICKEN EATING CORN, YOU ARE OBSERVING A MODERN DINOSAUR.

GLOSSARY

ASTEROID EXPLANATION—The theory that an asteroid impact near the Yucatán Peninsula in Mexico 66 million years ago caused the mass extinction of the dinosaurs.

BODY FOSSILS—The most common kind of fossils found. They are formed from the remains of dead animals and plants.

CRETACEOUS—The last period of the Mesozoic Era. It spanned 79 to 80 million years and lasted from about 145 to 66 million years ago.

CT SCANS—A CT or CAT (computerized tomography) scan provides a three-dimensional look into the internal parts of fossils.

DINOSAURS—A large group of ancient reptiles that ranged in size from small chickens to over 100-foot-long giants.

DINOSAUR TRACKS—Fossilized dinosaur footprints.

FOSSILS—The prehistoric remains, impressions, or traces of any once-living animal or plant.

HETEROTHERMS—Animals that have a temperature that changes depending on their activity.

HOT-BLOODED—Having a body temperature that remains about the same, regardless of one's surroundings. Mammals and birds are usually warm-blooded.

IRIDIUM—A very hard, silvery white metallic element. Its periodic table symbol is *Ir*.

JURASSIC—The middle period of the Mesozoic Era that stretched from about 201 to about 145 million years ago. Plant-eating dinosaurs such as the sauropods and meat-eating dinosaurs such as *Allosaurus* roamed the land.

K-T BOUNDARY—The geological point between the Cretaceous and Tertiary Periods. It is characterized by the extinction of the dinosaurs and many other forms of life.

MAMMALS—Warm-blooded animals that have hairy or furry bodies.

MASS EXTINCTION—A widespread and rapid decrease in the number of animal species.

MEAT-EATERS—A carnivore that eats the flesh of animals.

MELANOSOMES—Parts of a cell that are responsible for color in an animal's appearance.

MESOZOIC ERA—An interval of time between about 252 to about 66 million years ago. It is sometimes known as the Age of Reptiles.

PALEONTOLOGISTS—Scientists who study fossils.

PANGAEA—A supercontinent that included all of Earth's current continents in one large mass.

PLANT-EATERS—An animal that eats vegetation such as grasses, leaves, flowers, and seeds.

PLATE TECTONICS—A theory in which Earth's crust is divided into a number of large plates, each of which moves independently and may collide, slide over or under, or move past neighboring plates.

SAUROPODS—A class of dinosaurs with very long necks and tails, small heads, and four thick, pillarlike legs. Sauropods were some of the largest land animals ever, which included *Brontosaurus* and *Diplodocus*.

SEDIMENTARY ROCKS—Types of rock that are formed by the gradual accumulation of small mineral particles on the floor of oceans or other bodies of water.

THEROPODS—A group of carnivorous dinosaurs, such as *T. rex*, which walked or ran on their large hind legs.

TRACE FOSSILS—A fossil of a footprint, trail, or other trace of an animal rather than the animal itself.

TRIASSIC—The earliest period of the Mesozoic Era, which lasted from about 252 to 201 million years ago.

VOLCANO EXPLANATION—A massive eruption of volcanoes over many years that choked the skies with dust and starved plants of the sun's energy. This resulted in the death of plants, then the death of dinosaurs that ate plants, and, eventually, the death of dinosaurs that ate animals (although some small mammals survived). This is one of two theories about the cause of dinosaur extinction. The other theory is called the asteroid explanation.

BAROSAURUS

INDEX

FOR FURTHER READING

- *Dinosaurs: A Visual Encyclopedia (2nd edition)* by DK Publishing (DK Children's, 2018)
- *National Geographic Kids Ultimate Dinopedia (Second Edition)* by Don Lessem, illustrated by Franco Tempesta (National Geographic Children's Books, 2017)
- *Absolute Expert: Dinosaurs* by Lela Nargi with Steve Brusatte (National Geographic Children's Books, 2018)

AQUILOPS

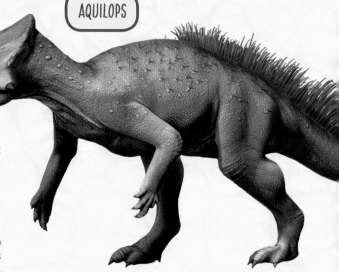